C000171417

TAKING

PART

A School Newspaper

009017/371.8974

HEWITT S

A school newspaper

£10.99

by S

tograph

**Books are to be returned on or before
the last date below.**

LIBREX —

© 2002 Franklin Watts

First published in 2002 by
Franklin Watts
96 Leonard Street
LONDON
EC2A 4XD

Franklin Watts Australia
56 O'Riordan Street
Alexandria
NSW 2015

ISBN: 0 7496 4369 2
Dewey Decimal Classification 371.8
A CIP catalogue reference for this book is available from the British
Library.

Printed in Malaysia

Editor: Kate Banham
Designer: Joelle Wheelwright
Art Direction: Peter Scoulding
Photography: Chris Fairclough

Acknowledgements
The publishers would like to thank the staff and pupils of Southwold
Primary School, Radford, Nottingham, for their help in the production
of this book. The photograph on page 25 is reproduced by kind
permission of Jarrold Publishing.

Contents

(Words printed in **bold italics** are explained in the glossary.)

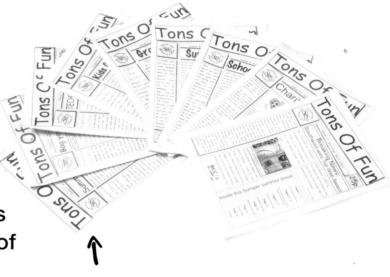

When Southwold Primary School bought its first computer, the children decided to use it to make a school newspaper. The newspaper was a great success. The readers asked for more and 'Tons of Fun' was born. The latest *edition* is number 11!

The first edition of 'Tons of Fun' was given away free – now it costs 25p.

The school was built about 30 years ago.

School and community

Southwold School is in Radford in the city of Nottingham. People who live in Radford can read 'Tons of Fun' to find out what the children are doing inside their school and outside in the *community*. The newspaper helps the school and the community to keep in touch.

Getting to know us

If you want to find out about Southwold, you can read the school **_prospectus_**, visit the school website or arrange a visit. But if you want up-to-date news and comments written by the children, then the place to look is the school newspaper.

Parents look forward to getting the latest edition.

Southwold school prospectus gives lots of official information about the school.

Award!

'Tons of Fun' has won an award. The Daily Telegraph ran a competition for the best school newspaper, and 'Tons of Fun' won the highly commended award.

What the children say:

I like to read our newspaper because I like to keep informed about what's happening around the school.

Our school newspaper keeps you up with the latest news.

Page by Page

'Tons of Fun' is *produced* by the children at school, from beginning to end. It usually has 8 pages of news, *interviews*, pictures, information, quizzes and puzzles. The latest bumper edition has 12 pages.

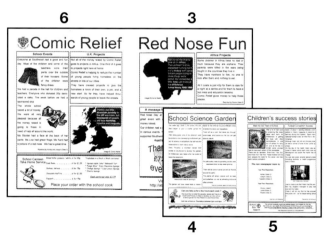

Two printed sheets are put together to make one 8-page newspaper.

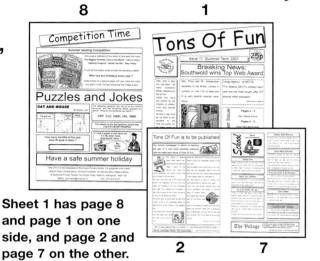

Sheet 1 has page 8 and page 1 on one side, and page 2 and page 7 on the other.

Sheet 2 has page 6 and page 3 on one side, and page 4 and page 5 on the other.

front page news

An exciting *headline* on the front will make you want to buy the paper and read more. The headline 'Southwold wins Top Web Award' announced exciting news. Website pages the school made for Comic Relief 2001 won the British Educational and Communication Technology Agency – BECTa – award.

↑ The whole school helped to create the winning web pages so everyone wanted to read the story.

Inside pages

Pages 2 to 6 are packed with reports, interviews and photographs. On page 4, the school cook advertises the School Canteen Take Home Service – delicious freshly-baked cookies and cakes at a very good price!

'These cakes smell delicious.' ↓

News and information

If you don't read page 7, you will miss out on interesting school news, important information and special requests.

- A book is going to be written about Southwold School newspaper.
- Don't miss the Nursery cake sale.
- Please bring in postcards for the internet geography project.

'I know the answer to this one.' ↑

Questions

If your school produced a newspaper, what would you like to read in it?

What would you put in to make sure everyone wanted to buy the paper?

competition time

On the back page there are puzzles and jokes for all ages and a competition with great prizes. Could you answer this question: 'Who has two birthdays every year?' The winner of this competition won 5 books to read for the summer holidays.

The Editorial Team

The success of 'Tons of Fun' depends on the hard work of year 5 teacher, Mr Widdowson, and the *editorial team*. Everyone who is interested volunteers, and Mr Widdowson chooses the 6 members of the team – 3 from year 4 and 3 from year 5. Together they plan and produce the newspaper.

The editorial team have fun working together. ↑

'We all work together to produce each issue of the newspaper.' ↓

I'd bought all the newspapers and they looked fun, so I wanted to do one.

Training

Members of the editorial team can take part in producing as many as 6 editions of 'Tons of Fun', so they have plenty of expertise. When they move on, they train a new team to take their place.

Editorial skills

All the members of the editorial team agree that they need certain skills in order to do their jobs well. These are the skills they feel are most important.

- Write fast
- Know how to use a computer
- Do thorough research
- Enjoy working as a team

'You need to write fast so you can do it all at dinner time.'

'You need computer skills, and you need to be able to use the internet to find out lots of things.'

'Three of us write up the same report, then we take the best from each report and write it again.'

Questions

Would you have the skills to be a member of the editorial team?

Why do you think the editorial team have fun working together?

Editorial Meetings

At the beginning of every term, the team get together with Mr Widdowson to plan the newspaper. They look at a list of the major events of the term and discuss which ones will make good stories. Then they plan what should go on each page.

↑ Editorial meetings are fun.

Last minute

A template of the paper is put up on the computer and gradually filled in. Sometimes spaces remain blank until the last minute because news comes in just before the newspaper goes to press.

Tons Of Fun

Issue   Term 200   25p

Inside this Issue
Pages 2-3
Page 4-5
Page 6
Page 7
School News
Page 8
Quizzes

↗

The newspaper starts as a blank template.

When we go to our first meeting, we decide what's going on the middle pages and the front page and the other pages.

Changes

You never know what will happen in the news, so the team meet every two weeks. They often have to change the position of the stories and find new material.

fast thinking

At one meeting, the team planned a whole page on a visit to the school by an author and illustrator of children's books. When the visit was cancelled, they had to think fast to fill in the spaces.

'What shall we write about instead?'

Red Nose Day

The big event of term was going to be Red Nose Day, so the team decided it should be headline news on the front page and should fill the centre pages too. Luckily, everything went according to plan this time!

Red Nose Day was a great success.

Good stories help to sell newspapers and attract new readers. The 'Tons of Fun' editorial team is always on the look-out for a story that everyone will want to read. They aim to reach as many readers as they can.

Get your copy of 'Tons of Fun'!

Everyone was excited about the good news.

How much?

'Tons of Fun' costs 25p but it doesn't make a profit. All the money goes towards the cost of production.

Scoop!

Exciting news had broken in the staff room – two members of staff were expecting babies at almost the same time. They decided to keep it a secret from the children and announce the news in the next edition of 'Tons of Fun'. Once the news had broken, everyone wanted to buy a copy and read all about it!

Prizes

The competitions on the back page help to sell the newspaper. Everyone wants to have a go at winning the prizes. The names of all the children who got the right answer are put into a box. During assembly, the head teacher, Mrs Price, draws out the winning name.

'And the competition winner is …'

'Congratulations!'

If you write about something in the newspaper then everybody will know about it.

Champion

Hardly anybody knew that one of the boys in class 3 was going to Taekwondo classes until he made headline news by winning third prize in a national championship. The school was very proud of him. Now the whole school knows – and now they also know that Taekwondo is a self-defence martial art.

School Champion

Class 3 has a champion hiding away within the class.

One boy made front page news by winning a prize in a national Taekwondo championship.

Interviewing

A reporter needs to be good at doing interviews. Each question has to be carefully thought out so that the answers are interesting and full of information. A 'yes' or 'no' answer is very boring!

Trip to the zoo

The editorial team always try to get their interviews immediately after an event when everyone's memory is still fresh. When the Infants went on a trip to Twycross Zoo, the team prepared some questions and interviewed the children the very next morning.

Here are the questions they asked:
- What animals did you see?
- What animals did you like?
- Was it fun?
- What day did you go?
- How did you get there?

Q: How did you get there?
A: On the bus. We went to sleep on the way back.

Q: What animals did you like?
A: I liked Jo the gorilla.

NETHER STOWE SCHOOL LIBRARY

A book about the newspaper!

The editorial team decided to report that this book was being produced. When they first heard about it, they printed the news on page 7 of issue 10 (right).

Read all about it

Our newspaper just keeps getting better and bette... A publisher has asked whether we would like to p... lish a book all about how to make a newspaper in ... school. Watch this space for further details.

Reported by Mr. Widdowson

Good news for Korky fans

Korky Paul will be coming to Southwold to meet the children during the morning of the 28th June.

After the author's first two visits, they wrote a full report on the progress of the book so far and printed it in issue 11 (left).

Tons Of Fun is to be published

Our school newspaper is about to become the star of a new book showing everyone how we make each issue of Tons Of Fun.

BIG NEWS

The author of several books, Sally Hewitt, contacted Southwold after she made a search on the Internet and found our school newspaper. She spoke to Mrs Price and arranged to visit the school.

She had a quick tour around the school and spoke to Mr Widdowson and Mrs Price. She asked Mr Widdowson how the newspaper was made, from meeting with the editors to plan what is going into each issue, through to printing off and selling the copies.

She came back to school after the half term holiday to talk to the newspaper editors as well as some of the readers of the newspaper.

When she spoke to the editors she asked them what they had to do for each issue.

Nicole told Sally that the editors were responsible for writing the newspaper reports on the computers.

She also asked some infants and juniors why they read the newspaper. Most of the children told her they liked the last page because of the puzzles, jokes and competitions.

She also spoke to a group of children who had helped write the fashion show report.

When she had finished asking about the school newspaper she spoke to another group of children about the projects they had created for the school website.

Sally will be visiting Southwold one more time before the summer holiday with a photographer to take some pictures that will then go into the book. This will be sold all around the country.

Reported by Natasha and Joseph

The author talked to the school about writing non-fiction books for children.

Seven hund... t...nty four.

Then the editorial team interviewed the author.

Questions

Which authors would you like to visit your school?

What questions would you ask them?

The Big Story

Each issue of 'Tons of Fun' carries a big story. In issue 11 the big story was about the school winning a top web award, in issue 10 it was Red Nose Day and in issue 8 the big story headline was Super Models.

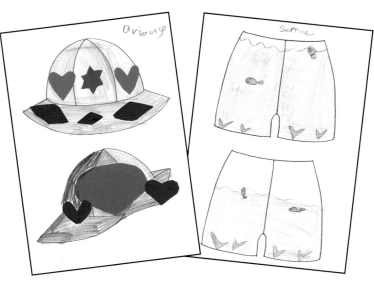

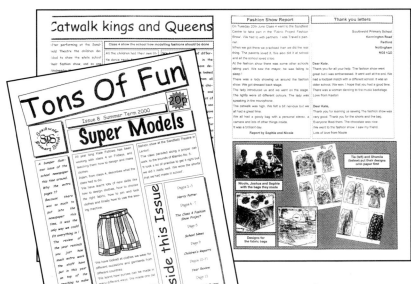

↑ **The newspaper report told the whole story of the fabric project from beginning to end.**

fabric project

Class 4 had been learning how to design and make their own clothes. The climax of their year's work was to model their clothes at a fashion show. 'Tons of Fun' devoted the front page and the centre pages to the story.

Class 4

Only the children from class 4 were involved, but the whole school, their families and anyone else who bought the newspaper could read about the fun they had doing the project.

Telling the story

The editorial team did a good job. They made sure everyone in class 4 made a contribution to the report. Nothing was left out. Their writing brought the story alive and it was exciting to read.

The editorial team's report on the fabric project made you feel as if you had been there yourself.

Class 4 talked about what they liked best about the fashion project.

> When I was making the patchwork bag, especially the leaves.

> When I was on the catwalk and all the lights were flashing.

> When someone's shorts were falling down in the catwalk show!

Class 4 put on their fashion show for the whole school.

The models danced down the catwalk to loud music.

Going to Press

When all the reports have been written and the pictures added to the template on the computer, a rough copy of the whole newspaper, called a *proof*, is printed. The proof is checked for mistakes by several members of staff.

Mistakes are marked with a highlighter pen. →

copyright

If pictures and articles used in the paper have this *copyright* symbol © it means that the editorial team have had to ask for permission to use them. They may even have had to pay a fee.

Master copy

When all the mistakes have been corrected on the computer and copyright has been checked, a master copy is printed. It has to be kept clean and smooth. Every single copy of this issue of 'Tons of Fun' will be made from just one master copy.

 Everything has been checked, now printing can begin.

Production line

The editorial team take their place on the production line. They are going to print 100 copies of a bumper edition to sell at sports day. If they sell all the copies at 25p each, they will make £25.

First the master copy is carefully put in place.

Next, sheets of clean A3 paper are fed into the photocopier. Each sheet is printed on both sides.

The printed sheets are folded and put together in the right order.

The crisp new copies are put into a box ready to be sold to eagerly waiting readers.

The Readers

Southwold pupils are not the only readers of 'Tons of Fun'. They take it home for their parents, grandparents and friends to read. It is even sold along with all the other papers at the nearby newsagent.

> I take it round to my grandma's because she likes to read the newspaper.

'Good. More copies of "Tons of Fun". We've just sold out!'

circulation

A newspaper's *circulation* is how many copies are sold. Southwold hopes to increase the circulation of 'Tons of Fun'. If local people read it they will get to know more about the school. They might offer to help the school, or perhaps they may think of a way the school can help them.

Grandma reads the paper to one of the nursery children.

'I haven't finished reading it yet!'

Mum likes looking to see if my work got in the paper – she's proud.

Questions

What do you think your family would enjoy about reading your school newspaper?

What could you put in a school newspaper to make sure local people wanted to read it?

My younger sister is on the editorial team. I read the paper to see if she's better at writing than me.

I like the jokes and sometimes I like to tell my friend who doesn't live near me any more. I phone her up and tell her the jokes.

The children have all kinds of different reasons for reading the paper.

On-line

Four weeks after the newspaper has been published, after everyone has had a chance to buy their copy, it is posted on the school website. Check it out on http://atschool.eduweb.co.uk/southwold/newspaper.htm. You can read copies of the paper right back to issue 3 absolutely free!

↑ Every issue of 'Tons of Fun' is posted on the Southwold website.

Lucas will be able to read the newspaper, even when he is thousands of miles away. ↑

Lucas

Lucas has been at Southwold for a year and he has made a lot of friends. This summer, he is going back to South America. He says he will visit the school website and read the latest edition of the newspaper. It will be a good way of keeping in touch.

Browsing

Someone visiting the school website to read 'Tons of Fun' might find themselves browsing through some of the other web pages on the site. There are all kinds of interesting pages to go to. How about taking a tour of the city of Nottingham?

↑ There are so many pages on the website, there is sure to be something that interests you.

Nottingham
This is my City

An ambitious local study project by the children in class 3. 02/00

* Geography
* History
* Landmarks
* Locals
* Ballads of Robin Hood
* Introduction to the Ballads
* The tale of Maid Marion
* The tale of Little John
* The tale of Friar Tuck
* The tale of Alan a Dale
* The tale of Robin and the Potter
* The tale of the Silver Arrow
* The tale of Robin and the Monk
* The tale of Robin's Last Arrow

Robin Hood is a legendary
figure from Nottingham.

Linking Up

 Southwold can share and celebrate school news, display the children's work and publish information instantly by posting it on their website. The school has made links with people all over the country and abroad through the website.

↑ **The website has had over 2,000 hits!**

Students from abroad have contacted the school through the guest book and asked if they can do a teaching practice there. ↑

Guest book

You can often find a guest book in famous buildings where visitors can sign their names and write comments. Southwold website has a guest book page where visitors can write a message for everyone to read. The children e-mail their replies.

The Village

The Village is a literacy project originally devised by Mr Widdowson. Now schools all over the UK take part. First, Southwold pupils created a map of a fictional village. Then various different schools chose an area to be responsible for. Children from each school have written descriptions of their chosen area and can now devise stories about the characters who live there.

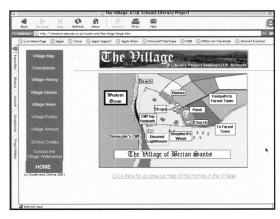

Groups of children who have never met each other work on The Village project.

The opening page of The Village project.

I visit the website every weekend to see if there are any new things on it. I like to look at The Village.

It's good for the school to have a good website. Everyone can keep in touch with what's going on.

Questions

If your school had a website, what do you think should be put on it?

Why do you think it's a good idea for a school to have a website?

In touch

Both the website and 'Tons of Fun' make sure that everyone can find out what's going on at Southwold School – and have fun doing it.

Glossary

Circulation   Newspapers and magazines sell as many copies as they can. The number of copies they sell is their circulation. The more copies sold, the bigger the circulation.

Community   The community is the people who live together in a neighbourhood. Southwold school is in the community of Radford.

Copyright   Permission must be asked for if you want to copy anything with this copyright symbol ©. You may have to pay a fee.

Edition   Each new production of a paper is a new edition. Some papers bring out a new edition every day, some once a week. A new edition of 'Tons of Fun' comes out once a term.

Editorial team   The newspaper editorial team are responsible for planning each edition, writing the articles and producing the finished copies.

Headline   A newspaper headline is at the top of the front page or an article. It is in big, bold print and tells the reader what the article is about.

Interview   For a newspaper interview, a journalist asks someone questions and then writes up a report using information from their answers.

Production   Newspaper production is all the work done from the first idea to printing the latest edition.

Proof   A proof is a rough copy of a newspaper. Changes can be made and mistakes can be put right on the proof.

Prospectus   A school prospectus is information about the school. The information is usually printed in a booklet that can be given to new pupils and their parents.

Taking Part

Produce a school newspaper

Southwold School produces a newspaper that is popular with pupils, parents and teachers. Now they even sell in their local community.

Produce one edition of a school newspaper. Ask your readers what they think of it and if they have any ideas. Make your second edition even better than the first.

Visit your local newspaper

Buy and read your local newspaper. It will be full of stories and information about your community.

Arrange a visit to the newspaper offices. It's a good way to meet editors and journalists and learn about how a newspaper is produced.

Interview someone special

'Tons of Fun' editorial team interview children, visitors and all kinds of interesting people for their newspaper.

Interview someone who has just done something interesting. Prepare a list of good questions to make sure you get all the information you want.

Be a reporter

'Tons of Fun' reports on all Southwold School's special events. People can all read about them, even if they didn't take part.

Write up a report on your next school visit. Don't forget to take notes and collect all the information you can to help remember what happened. You could even take a camera.

Index

NETHER STOWE
SCHOOL LIBRARY